Alessandro Serenelli

Alessandro Serenelli

A Story of Forgiveness

CHARLES D. ENGEL

Our Sunday Visitor
Huntington, Indiana

Our Sunday Visitor Publishing Division
Our Sunday Visitor, Inc.
200 Noll Plaza
Huntington, IN 46750
www.osv.com
1-800-348-2440

ISBN: 978-1-68192-558-5 (Inventory No. T2438)
1. BIOGRAPHY & AUTOBIOGRAPHY—Religious.
2. BIOGRAPHY & AUTOBIOGRAPHY—General. 3. RELIGION—Christianity—Catholic.

eISBN: 978-1-68192-559-2
LCCN: 2019954610

Cover design: Tyler Ottinger
Cover art: copyright Fr. Carlos Martins; used with permission
Interior design: Amanda Falk
Interior art: copyright Fr. Carlos Martins; used with permission. / Shutterstock / Saint Maria Goretti (1976), Theodore C. Barbarossa. © Basilica of the National Shrine of the Immaculate Conception, Washington, D.C.; used with permission.

PRINTED IN THE UNITED STATES OF AMERICA

for Imelda
my wife, my love

Alessandro Serenelli visiting with Assunta Goretti, the mother of Maria, after his release from prison. Assunta forgave her daughter's murderer, just as Maria herself had forgiven him. Copyright Fr. Carlos Martins.

"I forgive him, and I want him to be with me in heaven."
Saint Maria Goretti

"In the heroic testimony of (Saint Maria Goretti), her forgiveness of the man who killed her and her desire to be able to meet him one day in heaven deserves special attention. This spiritual and social message is of extraordinary relevance in our time. ... Maria Goretti's murderer recognized the sin he had committed. He asked forgiveness of God, and of the martyr's family, conscientiously expiated his crime and lived the rest of his life in this spiritual frame of mind."

Saint John Paul II,
letter to the Bishop of Albano
on the centenary of the death of Saint Maria Goretti,
July 6, 2002

Contents

Alessandro Serenelli kneels in prayer before an image of Saint Maria Goretti, who became his special patron. Copyright Fr. Carlos Martins.

Introduction

It has always been told as *her* story. The story of Maria Goretti, an angelic eleven-year-old murdered by her neighbor as she struggled to defend her chastity. Alessandro Serenelli, a young man just one month out of his teens, killed Maria because she would not accommodate his demands. After years of popular veneration and exhaustive investigation on the part of the Church, Maria was canonized. She was celebrated as a champion of chastity, the virtue for which she died. Alessandro too came to be remembered — for his heinous crime. Despite how the story has been told, however, it was never just *her* story. With her words of forgiveness toward Alessandro Serenelli, Maria Goretti herself assured it could never be so, nor would she have wanted it to be. In fact, it has always been *their* story.

Crimes such as Alessandro's — an unsuccessful sexual assault, this one ending in a brutal murder — often make the nightly news, if only on the local outlet. Unfortunate victims and their assailants have their fifteen minutes in the blinding glare of the media's spotlight. Then, outside of a relatively small circle of family and friends, the tragedy is forgotten. It becomes yesterday's news, all too soon to be replaced by an all too similar story.

This was not the case with *their* story.

The tragic death of Maria Goretti was first reported in the tabloids of her day. She was killed in 1902, and Alessandro Serenelli and his monstrous actions became fodder for the tabloids. Sensationalism sells newspapers, and this story qualified, being both brutal and lurid enough to guarantee coverage.

There was, however, an important fact or two that escaped the news coverage of the crime. It was not reported that eleven-year-old Maria Goretti, in the midst of the horrendous attack, admonished her attacker to consider his own soul, his own salvation. Nor did the newspapers report that Maria, just hours later on her deathbed, said she not only forgave Alessandro Serenelli, but that she wanted him one day to be with her in heaven.

Though the newspaper coverage lasted for several days, there are no interviews with Assunta Goretti, the girl's mother. It was Assunta Goretti who could have told them of her daughter's final words. So too could have the priest, Don Temistocle Signori, who ministered to Maria at the end. He could have repeated words that were addressed directly to him, words that were not part of a sacramental confession. The Goretti family's neighbor and friend Teresa Cimarelli, present at the child's deathbed to support Maria's mother, had also heard the child's words: "I forgive him, and I want him to be with me in heaven."

Over time these extraordinary words of pardon were often repeated, first by those who themselves had heard them spoken. These words of mercy made this sexual assault quite different from similar stories in the news. While Alessandro Serenelli succeeded in taking Maria Goretti's physical life, she was determined to preserve his spiritual life. It was the little girl's words of forgiveness that, from the first, kept the story of Maria Goretti and Alessandro Serenelli alive beyond the attention span of the press. It would be these words of mercy that would propel Maria Goretti's popular cult and eventual canonization. And it was this mercy eventually accepted by her murderer — though it would take years — that now propels the nascent cult of Alessandro Serenelli.

The word "cult" can have a dark and sinister connotation. Today it is often associated with a fad or a fanatical following of a false and even harmful practice or philosophy. But there is an older application of the word, used to characterize pre-Christian worship and rituals. In its use throughout the pagan world, the word *cultus* had a sacred connotation — sacred, that is, as the pagan world worshiped. In that world, worship was afforded even living men, most prominently the worship of the emperor. As a word connoting worship, however, it was natural that it be appropriated by the early Church for inclusion in her own lexicon. Scholars such as Peter Brown in *The Cult of the Saints: Its Rise and Function in Latin Christianity* and, perhaps even more so, Allen Brent in *The Imperial Cult and the Development of Church Order* are careful to show how the meaning of *cultus* was radically transformed in the Christian understanding. Worship for the Christian belonged to God alone.

The veneration of the saints, early on reserved to the martyrs, was the form of cult afforded Our Lady and the saints. Saint John Chrysostom in the fourth century authored *The Cult of the Saints*. The Church still preserves the word *cultus*, sanctifying it, Christianizing it, by its application to those sacred actions, both public and private — including the Mass — that give praise and glory to God, and that demonstrate the Christian's love of those holy ones who are now with God in heaven.

What is sometimes referred to in Catholicism as a saint's "cult" encompasses many aspects. Paramount to a saint's cult is his or her liturgical feast. This is an annual observance, the saint's feast day, on which the saint's memorial Mass is celebrated by the Church. It is paramount because during a saint's feast day Mass his or her link to Christ himself is most fully demonstrated, particularly in the Mass prayers composed for the feast day. These prayers articulate the heroic example of the saint as having witnessed to the Gospel in his or her earthly life. As a saint's feast day liturgy calls to mind the saint's virtues, we the faithful are called, in our own unique circumstances, to imitate their example.

But there are other, lesser aspects to a saint's cult. In the broader sense, a saint's cult refers to how the Church has promoted him or her, and how the faithful have received back the saint. That's right: *received back*. It is the faithful who first promote, or propose, to the Church a candidate for canonization, trusting Church officials to do what an individual, for all practical purposes, cannot do — that is, to put in the time and energy to objectively evaluate the sanctity of an individual. Devotion to a saint begins with the recognition by an individual Catholic, or a group of Catholics, that there is something about this person that is spiritually attractive. That attractiveness is holiness itself.

Again, as the wording of his or her feast day's liturgical prayers intend, the recollection of the saint's virtue invites us to consider our own witness as Jesus' disciples. Yet, be warned: How one saint or other was Christlike will surely not be the same for anyone else in the particulars. Instead, we each must find the measure of our own fidelity to the Gospel, sometimes in ordinary ways, and sometimes in extraordinary ways. To anyone who has ever flipped through a collection of saints' lives, this is evident. We find homemakers, artists, royalty, mystics, monks, martyrs, and more. Rarely, however, does the evangelical witness of a Christian show itself as stunningly as it does in the life of Alessandro Serenelli, who relinquished a hardened heart and humbly accepted God's transforming grace. In coming to appreciate the relationship between Maria Goretti and Alessandro Serenelli, and the witness they, together, offer us, one word is particularly helpful. That word is *accompaniment*.

Accompaniment as a Christian principle is as old as the New Testament itself. In the Christian vocabulary, it does not mean to "go along with" in the sense of accepting another's point of view or what he or she is proposing to do or not do. As Pope Francis uses the term in his apostolic exhortation *Evangelii Gaudium*, accompaniment for the Christian means quite simply not to abandon. Accompaniment then, as Pope Francis intends it, means to travel with another on the other's spiritual journey. Accompaniment is a sustained Christian action, which means it is an action rooted both in hope and charity. While the one who accompanies in this sense desires a genuine and heartfelt response, accompaniment cannot be coercive. Christian accompaniment is patient, allowing God's grace to be received, or even to be refused.

Accompaniment is a pastoral principle. But its practice is not reserved to priests. In *Evangelii Gaudium*, Pope Francis says the Church should initiate "everyone … into this 'art of accompaniment'" (169). To underscore the scope of the inclusiveness he envisions, the pope goes on to say just who he intends by everyone: "priests, religious, and laity." And since accompaniment is truly a means of evangelizing and of re-evangelizing, its meaning or manner of application is not exclusively to be determined by scholars, apologists, or canonists. It is not a technical word to be parsed and nuanced, but a deeply practical word that is meant to be lived.

Accompaniment is a guiding principle, not a dogmatically definable truth. As such it must forgo the safeguards requisite to protecting doctrinal integrity. To be sure, Sacred Scripture does not tell us to throw caution to the wind. It does, however, command courage. Pope Francis says that accompaniment requires that we "remove our sandals before the sacred ground of the other" (*EG* 169). As Christians, we know that we face daily opportunities to offer accompaniment, or to accept it, and these opportunities require varying degrees of courage. Thus God calls us to courage throughout Scripture: "Be not afraid."

As of this writing, and for several decades, the Church has been confronted with a clergy sexual abuse crisis. As Scripture reminds us that when one member of the body is in pain, the whole body suffers. All of us are affected. Many have been personally affected, and their pain has invaded our own being. Saint Peter once asked Jesus: "'Lord, how often shall my brother sin against me, and I forgive him? As many as seven times?' Jesus said to him, 'I do not say to you seven times, but seventy times seven'" (Mt 18:21–22). For the Church today, these words of Jesus may seem all the harder to hear.

The scandals the Church faces today seem to be unprecedented in the Church's long history. There is no apparent, satisfying answer as to how things could have gone so wrong for so long, with the abuse of minors not being decisively addressed. It appears that this refusal to address the abuse was intended only to protect the abusers and the reputation of the Church. As Christians, as with men and women of conscience universally, we have an innate sense of compassion for victims of any kind. They deserve our compassion. Yet, are we as Christians, whether in our anguish or even in our anger, justified in withholding forgiveness? Are there sins too great to be forgiven? As hard as it may be to accept, the answer is no — at least not for God, who is all-just yet all-merciful. Made in his image, we must, as best we can, forgive as he forgives. Where both sin and crime have conspired, both forgiveness and justice are our only hope.

In recalling Alessandro Serenelli, it is hoped that we may come to appreciate not only the roles forgiveness and justice played in his life, but their roles in our own lives. He came to recognize and accept that his victim truly desired his spiritual well-being. He came to see Maria Goretti as accompanying him to a peace he himself had lost hope of ever reaching. It is hoped that in coming to know Alessandro Serenelli, we may come to see that the Christian life is always a life of accompaniment, both in coming to pardon others, and in coming to accept the pardon of others.

There are no photographs of the young Alessandro — not even a mug shot from the time of his arrest. In the above, he is shown at Macarata, in the Capuchin monastery where he ended his days in prayer and penance. Copyright Fr. Carlos Martins.

Chapter One

Alessandro Serenelli:
Early Life (1882–1902)

Alessandro Serenelli was born on June 2, 1882, in Paterno d'Ancona, Italy. He was baptized the following day in Santa Maria Assunta, the parish church. Six years later he would be confirmed in the same church. His parents, Giovanni Serenelli and Cecilia Mengoni, had eight children, two of whom died in infancy. Alessandro was the last to be born. His parents earned their living as farmers, though they were never very successful, and the family seemed doomed to live in abject poverty.

Cecilia suffered greatly from stress, which eventually came to be recognized as mental illness. Her decline was precipitated by a tragedy that befell her son Gaspare. At thirteen, the boy was fortunate enough to be admitted to a minor seminary, not intending to be ordained, but as a boarding student. This opportunity held the great promise that only the luxury of an excellent education could hold. Sadly, while he was alone in the chapel during Eucharistic adoration at school, Gaspare was struck by an epileptic seizure. It damaged his brain, and he ended his days institutionalized in a mental asylum in 1885.

Feeling shamed, the mother began to show signs of a mental disorder. Once, while she was not in her right mind, she decided that it would be better for her youngest son to die, rather than possibly suffer a similar fate to that of Gaspare. She attempted to drown three-year-old Alessandro in a well. Her grotesque plan was only thwarted when her oldest son, Pietro, happened on the scene and prevented Alessandro's demise. In 1890, Cecilia was remanded to the insane asylum in Ancona, the same institution in which Gaspare had died.

When Alessandro was six, his father enrolled him in the local school. While his formal education lasted only a year and a half, during that short time he learned to read and write. These skills set him apart from most of his peers and would be a source of mixed blessings for him throughout his life.

In 1894, Giovanni Serenelli moved from Paterno d'Ancona to nearby Torrette. Alessandro, still only a boy, set out on his own, living along the Adriatic coast. He was attracted to the sea, and he mingled with the seafaring men on the wharfs and took on work among them. He would move from port to port, working as what might loosely be described as an apprentice longshoreman. Not yet a teenager, he spent his days and nights in the company of sailors and the moral unfortunates who inhabited the waterfront. Boys his own age who lived along the docks invited him to join them in visiting the brothels frequented by the sailors, or in viewing the pornographic images in which the sailors unashamedly took pleasure. Alessandro declined.

A few years later, at the time of his conviction for the murder and attempted rape of little Maria Goretti, he was accused of having used pornography. Alessandro denied this claim. The accusations arose because Assunta Goretti, Maria's mother, found certain images Alessandro pasted to his bedroom walls to be pornographic. They were images cut from the covers of popular journals, so while they might not have aligned with Assunta's moral views, they could not have been truly pornographic. When questioned at his trial about his access to pornography, Alessandro asked rhetorically, would the authorities allow pornography to be sold? The images he posted on his bedroom walls were of beautiful women, actresses, and singers. Some, he conceded, were scantily clad because they appeared in seaside scenes. Young Alessandro would have known firsthand the difference between pornography and tawdry photographs. The company of gruff men and boys who filled his youth, unanchored from home and family, assured that he knew the difference. These same men and boys had a corrosive effect on his character. His exposure to what can only be called a morally bankrupt lifestyle lasted five years.

While it may be that the influence of pornography has been too greatly credited in causing young Alessandro's moral decline, there is another cause that he acknowledged only in his later years. Instead of lewd images, it was reading that cast its spell over his imagination. It was in reading that Alessandro found his amusement and escape. As a boy and teen, his illiterate fellow workers mocked him for being able to read. In the ports through which he drifted, he could obtain cheap periodicals, newspapers, even used and dog-eared classic novels. When Alessandro eventually reunited with his father, Giovanni would bring his son newspapers and used books from Anzio and Nettuno. He would bring home to his son whatever he could afford, while he himself was unable to read even the titles.

In his advanced years, just before his death, Alessandro spoke of his eclectic reading habits. Some of the books he read in his early years were lurid and violent; others were lofty and heroic. He recalled that he once read a story somewhere in the writings of Stendhal, which included a vivid passage that particularly stayed with him. He liked reading graphic descriptions

— passages that he could see with his mind's eye. The Stendhal passage, he admitted, was the description of the violent murder of a young girl.

During Alessandro's trial for Maria's murder, the court-appointed psychiatrist evaluated him and determined that he had an above average intelligence. In her innocence, Assunta Goretti assumed that pornographic images were Alessandro's downfall. Alessandro's pornography was not what she had perceived. Rather, he had found what the illiterates who mocked him could not find as they fantasized. As a young boy in his mid-teens, he could find in sentences and paragraphs, or perversely read into them, things he could develop mentally.

In 1897, Giovanni, a widower whose children were now on their own, migrated to Olevano Romano, an agricultural region thirty-five miles east of Rome. He had taken to alcohol, and without the company of wife or children, seemed destined to failure. Seeing their father decline, Pietro contacted his brother Alessandro and encouraged him to abandon his vagabond life and go to the aid of their father. Fifteen-year-old Alessandro did just that.

Olevano Romano is a picturesque region. Small farms and olive groves abound. There, Giovanni and Alessandro found work on an estate owned by a Genoese landowner, a Protestant bishop named Cappellini. But the landowner was difficult, and the Serenellis soon moved on. By October 1898, the father and son found work in nearby Paliano. There they worked on land owned by Senator Giuseppe Scelsi and managed by his son.

In 1898, at Paliano, Giovanni and his son first met Luigi Goretti, his wife, Assunta, and their five children. The Gorettis too had migrated from near the Adriatic, from the hilltop town of Corinaldo. Arriving in Paliano in desperate search of work, they accepted employment on the large Scelsi farm. It was at Paliano that sixteen-year-old Alessandro first met nine-year-old Maria Goretti. From then on, their separate stories became *their* story. Eventually, just as at Olevano Romano, Giovanni found the overseer at Paliano overly demanding and Luigi Goretti concurred. The Serenelli and Goretti households soon moved on, but now partnered.

Count Attilio Mazzoleni needed laborers and sharecroppers on his estate in nearby Le Ferriere di Conca. The antithesis of Italy's famed and sunny tourist regions, the region that welcomed the two families was little more than a mosquito-ridden morass. It had been so for as long as history had recorded, and it would remain so until the first quarter of the twentieth century, when ways of permanently reclaiming the Pontine Marshes would transform the region into what is now a highly desirable Roman commuter suburb. Le Ferriere di Conca lies just thirty miles south of Rome, inland five miles from the Tyrrhenian coast of the Mediterranean Sea.

As sharecroppers for Count Mazzoleni, the Serenellis and

the Gorettis were housed under the same roof in a large two-story building. Originally, it served as an outbuilding, and the upper story had been a cheese factory. This upper story became the shared living quarters for the two families.

Fresco of Saint Maria Goretti in the Church of Saint Nicholas, Valencia, Italy.
jorisvo / Shutterstock.com

Chapter Two

Maria Goretti (1890–1902)

Maria Goretti was born on October 16, 1890, eight years after Alessandro Serenelli. Her parents were Luigi Goretti, an army veteran, and Assunta Carlini, a peasant orphaned in infancy. Both were devout Catholics. They lived in a modest stone cottage and earned their living as farmers. Their first child, a boy they named Antonio, died shortly after birth. Of the six children to survive infancy, Maria was the second oldest, and the first daughter. When it became evident that the family farm was not able to produce enough income, and that the house was far too small (being home also to Luigi's brother and his family), Luigi moved his family to Paliano. It would prove a poor alternative to picturesque Corinaldo.

In 1900, Teresa Goretti was born, the last of the Goretti children. That same year Luigi died of malaria. Before dying, he told his wife she should return the family to Corinaldo. She chose not to. Out of necessity, the widowed Assunta left the care of the household to Maria, freeing herself to do the more strenuous work in the fields. Maria was charged with the care of her siblings, four of whom were younger than she. Her responsibilities included the housework and cooking for both families, as well as all the other domestic chores usually entrusted to the mother. Maria was nine and a half years old.

In 1901, Maria received her first Communion. She had often entreated her mother to be allowed to receive the Sacrament. During those years, the usual age for children to receive their first Communion was twelve. Maria was not yet eleven. The parish priest, however, was impressed by Maria's genuine desire to receive holy Communion so it was arranged that she be prepared with other children from the area, receiving instruction at Count Mazzoleni's villa. The priest assured Assunta that her daughter was well prepared, and he allowed the child early reception of the Eucharist. As a present, Alessandro gave Maria the catechism he had received at the time of his own first Communion back in Torrette. He had managed to hold on to it even during his life along the docks. Maria, however, could neither read nor write.

Alessandro was the only member of the Goretti-Serenelli house-hold who was literate.

There is some question as to the date of Maria's first Com-munion. What is known is that by tradition, first Communion was celebrated each year at Conca on the feast of Corpus Christi in June. She received the Sacrament at the church at Conca, the Church of the Annunciation, which stood adjacent to Count Mazzoleni's villa. Before setting off for the church, wearing a borrowed red dress and her mother's earrings, she asked pardon of each member of the Goretti-Serenelli household for any of-fenses she may have committed.

In the months before Maria's first Communion, Alessandro made two sexual advances toward her. She refused both proposi-tions unequivocally. She did not tell her mother what had trans-pired for two reasons, which came to light only on her deathbed. First, she was concerned that her mother might pull up stakes to get away from the Serenellis and wander in hope of finding work elsewhere. Maria knew work was hard to find, and she did not want to add to her mother's burden. Also, she revealed to those at her hospital bedside that Alessandro had threatened her with death if she told anyone about the demands he made of her.

Then, on July 5, 1902, Alessandro left the work area where he, Maria's mother and siblings, along with some neighbors, were threshing beans. He excused himself and went back to the house. He knew he would find Maria alone save for the company of her youngest sister, Teresa, who was two years old. His own father was asleep in the shade under the exterior stone staircase. Alessandro climbed those stairs to enter the living quarters. Maria sat mending at the top of the steep stairway while Teresa slept at her feet. Alessandro demanded that Maria follow him into the kitchen. She refused. He pulled her into the kitchen and made his third attempt at convincing her to cooperate with him. Again, she refused. He stabbed her, wounding her many times, then left her for dead and locked himself in his bedroom. Maria, still alive, roused herself. Alessandro heard her. He returned to the kitchen and stabbed her several more times for a total of fourteen times. Then he locked himself in his room again, which would be a foretaste of prison.

Maria summoned enough strength to open the kitchen door and call for help. Young Teresa began to cry. Alessandro's father awoke and found what had happened. He called out to Maria's mother. Assunta, along with some neighbors and Maria's siblings, rushed to see what so disturbed the senior Serenelli. They found Maria bloodied and dying.

They sent for an ambulance and the police. Maria was taken by horse-drawn wagon to the hospital at Nettuno, seven miles away. Alessandro was placed in chains and walked to Nettuno between mounted officers.

Maria underwent hours of operation and without benefit of anesthesia because the doctors felt it might worsen her condition. Alessandro underwent an interrogation showing no signs of remorse.

Maria died the following day, July 6. Her agony lasted close to twenty-four hours. Before she died, she told her mother and those gathered around her bed the details of Alessandro's repeated proposals and threats. When Don Temistocle Signori, the parish priest, asked if she forgave her attacker, she told him that she did. What is more, she said she wanted her attacker to be with her in paradise. This extraordinary deathbed statement confirmed what many who knew her already believed to be true: Eleven-year-old Maria Goretti was a saint.

While living at Ascoli Piceno in the Capuchin friary there, Alessandro served as gardener and porter. It was at this door that he frequently greeted the curious who hoped for a glimpse of "the monster." Copyright Fr. Carlos Martins.

Chapter Three

Prison Sentence (1902–1929)

A lessandro, secured in iron wrist manacles, arrived at the Nettuno police station where he was interrogated and temporarily jailed before being transported to Regina Coeli prison in Rome where, on July 8, 1902, he made and signed a statement. That statement and other official police and court documents would be presented in Maria's process for canonization. They are included in the *positio*, the document prepared containing the testimonies and ancillary material prior to beatification, the penultimate step in the long process of canonization.

Alessandro's statement, made three days after his crime, bluntly describes the vileness of his plan. In part, it reads, "One day last June, taking advantage of the empty house, I tried to copulate with her, and lifted her skirt taking my erection from my pants." Then, detailing the events of July 5, he declared: "Taking her by the arm, I dragged Maria Goretti into the kitchen, closed and barred the door from the inside, and lifted Goretti's skirt from the front, not because I wanted to make an attempt on her honor but to get a better position to execute my plan, namely to make the tip of my weapon come in immediate contact with the body of Goretti without the obstruction of her clothes."

It is not surprising that there are people who attempt to explain why Alessandro, at barely twenty years of age, would ever commit such a heinous assault on an eleven-year-old girl. Was insanity a family trait? During Alessandro's trial, Dr. Giovanni Mingazzini, head of Rome's Lungara Psychiatry Hospital, examined him and determined that he was sane. The doctor also concluded that he possessed above average intelligence. Mingazzini allowed that Alessandro came from a home where mental health issues wreaked havoc, but he believed that the accused had been spared.

During Mingazzini's evaluation, Alessandro admitted that it was boredom compounded by the exhausting drudgery of his daily work that served as the impetus for his crime. He had read enough crime stories to reason that crime, in some perverse way, sometimes did pay. He reasoned that if he ultimately failed to convince Maria to agree to his sexual advances, if nothing else, he would have a better life in prison if he killed her. When, three months having lapsed since the murder, Mingazzini asked the accused if he had any remorse, he replied he didn't. He assured the doctor that had Maria Goretti consented, he would not have harmed her in the least.

On October 15, 1902, the eve of Maria's birthday, Alessandro was sentenced to thirty years in prison. He began serving his sentence at Regina Coeli, a Roman prison originally built as a convent, which had been appropriated by the Italian state in the late nineteenth century. The prison retains it religious name, Regina Coeli, Queen of Heaven, and still serves as a Roman prison. Alessandro spent his first three years in solitary confinement and the remaining in hard labor. One must wonder how Alessandro felt when the sentence sank in. If the boredom and harshness of his life as a sharecropper in the mosquito-infested Pontine Marshes had been the impetus to crime, how was prison life a better choice?

Alessandro Serenelli was to spend only four months in Regina Coeli. In February 1903, he was transferred to a penitentiary in Noto, Sicily. At Noto, he served out his time in solitary confinement, as ordered by the sentencing judge, laboring as a rope-maker and at other monotonous jobs.

In 1908, Alessandro, still unrepentant, experienced what came to be regarded as his moment of conversion. The change that radically transformed him began with a dream. In Matthew's Gospel, God spoke to Saint Joseph in a dream, urging him first to take the pregnant and unwed Virgin Mary as his wife. In dreams, Joseph was also told to flee into Egypt to escape Herod, and then later to abandon Egypt and return to his homeland. God can speak to us in dreams, and this is how he chose to reach Alessandro. In a dream, Maria Goretti visited Alessandro in his prison cell.

This dream came soon after another extraordinary event. At the end of December 1908, an earthquake shook Noto. The quake took the lives of over thirty thousand in neighboring Messina, and its shocks caused damage to the penitentiary. This disaster brought out religious fervor in many of the prisoners, who believed God spared them.

Days after the cataclysm, Alessandro had his dream. He said his cell became a garden, bright with sunshine. A beautiful girl dressed in white approached him and he realized it was Maria walking toward him without fear. This time the tables were turned. It was he who wanted to flee from her. Maria stood before Alessandro and presented white lilies she had gathered as she moved toward him. She handed them to him one by one. Each flower turned into a small flame as he grasped it. She gave him fourteen lilies, one for each of the wounds he inflicted on July 5, 1902. Alessandro awoke a changed man.

While Alessandro's new attitude was rewarded with better

treatment by the warden and the prison guards, his sentence was not shortened. The shortened sentence would come later.

In the autumn of 1910, the bishop of Noto, Giovanni Blandini, at the prompting of a fellow bishop and of Maria's earliest biographer, Carlo Marini, visited Alessandro. No doubt this was an extraordinary visit, for while prisons have chaplains, it is rare that a particular inmate would receive a visit from such an important clergyman. The bishop wanted more information about Maria, for devotion among the people for the young girl had never diminished. On the contrary Maria's popular cult was growing.

The bishop listened to Alessandro's story, which must have included the story of the dream he had had two years earlier. Bishop Blandini asked Alessandro to write something detailing his conversion, and how he remembered the facts regarding both Maria's opposition to his advances and his own state of mind at the time of the crime. Alessandro did so, dating a letter to Bishop Blandini November 10, 1910. The text of the letter, however, contains no written account of the dream that had awakened such a strong sense of remorse in him. It reads as follows:

> Most Reverend Excellency, I cannot sufficiently express the comfort my grieved being received from the honor of the conversation with your illustrious Excellency; for which I send you my gratitude without measure. If it be true that in

a strangely fated moment of mental aberration I was constrained, impelled by passion beyond my control to do an act of barbarous homicide, for which the law has already meted to me accorded punishment, I cannot fully accuse myself unconditionally and say that my act was solely and voluntarily for the purpose of doing so great an evil, because of my green age and my meager cognizance of mature life were the real causes for bringing me to the sorry pass which today I bitterly weep over. Multiplied is my weeping now my grown conscience tells me I have bereft the life of a poor innocent, who until the tragic end wished to save and maintain her virginal honor, sacrificing herself to a brutal death rather than to my desire, all of which fact has spun me into the terrible abyss. I publically (*sic*) detest my crime and ask forgiveness from God and also from the poor and desolate family of my victim. I want to hope that even I am able to obtain forgiveness like to many others on this earth. To you bishop I present the declaration of hope that even you will forgive me for the major evil done by the inexpert youth I was, and that your prayers will unite with mine to ask forgiveness for me

> from Him Who governs all, and may I receive
> a calm sea and benediction with my poor final
> extinction.
>   I respectfully kiss your hand and beg from
> you a feeling of forgiveness.
>
>   Alessandro Serenelli

Long before Alessandro wrote this letter, impressive expressions of the popular cult of Maria Goretti had begun to manifest themselves. First was an article published in October 1902, just three months after Maria's death, in *Figlie di Maria,* the monthly magazine of the sodalists of the Children of Mary. The publication had many subscribers across Italy and the Italian diaspora. A biography of Maria was published in 1904, complete with photographs (none of her). Also in 1904, an imposing marble monument was erected in the Passionists' church in Nettuno. The monument, done in high and low relief, even included the figure of Alessandro retreating to his room after having stabbed the child he failed to seduce.

In December 1910, a month after Alessandro wrote to the bishop of Noto, the pope, Saint Pius X, delivered a homily on the feast of the Immaculate Conception in which he extolled Maria. He referred to her as a new Saint Agnes, a virgin martyr of the early church. This was an almost incredible recognition of someone not yet even proposed for sainthood. Clearly, the pope recognized the popular cult that continued to gather steam.

During these years, Italy was fighting in northern Africa, site of its colonies. In 1915, Italy entered the tumult of World War I. As it turned out, prison proved a safe place for Alessandro. Inmates were not drafted into the military and so were spared the dangers and hardships of battle. Around this time, Alessandro requested transfer to another prison, one where farming was the primary industry of the inmates. He was told that the war made such a move impossible. He was relocated, however, to Syracuse, where he worked in a quarry. In 1918, while in Syracuse, he received news that his father had died in a poorhouse.

In 1919, with the war over, Alessandro was moved to Bitti, the site of an agricultural prison on the island of Sardinia. Finally he was doing work he knew. In 1924, Prisoner 3142, as the penal authorities identified Alessandro, was transferred one last time, this time to the southern city of Alghero, also on the island of Sardinia. Because of his good behavior, two years were commuted from Alessandro's sentence. Another year's reprieve was granted to select inmates on the occasion of the wedding of the king's son. In 1929, after twenty-seven years in prison, Alessandro was free.

That same year Maria's body was freed from its grave exhumed in anticipation of the opening of her cause for canonization. Maria's remains were transferred to the Passionist church at Nettuno. Alessandro went to live with his brother Pietro in Torrette.

Chapter Four

Starting Over (1929–1937)

Alessandro left prison wearing a suit his brother Pietro sent him. A prison official escorted him from Sardinia to Rome. There, for a pre-release debriefing, he spent several days in Regina Coeli. He was told that even in freedom, he would not be totally at liberty; the local police would keep track of his whereabouts. Alessandro would have to adhere to a curfew and was not to be part of any gatherings.

With these instructions, he was given a rail ticket and headed for Torrette and the home of his brother Pietro and his family. They had offered to welcome him into their home.

A free man again, Alessandro soon found work but was quickly let go. He could not escape his past. Each time the locals learned his identity, there were problems. After all, he was a child murderer. What is more, the girl he killed back in 1902 was now part of Italian lore, and news of her advancement toward beatification was often in the newspapers. Maria was already considered a saint. Alessandro was a curiosity, and a despised curiosity at that.

While living in Torrette, Alessandro witnessed the love Pietro and his wife, Maria, had for their children. Maria was kind to him, too. Alessandro would speak of her as the only woman who gave him respect in these years. Getting to know his sister-in-law caused him to speculate that perhaps his wayward youth would have been different if he had received love from his mother.

In early November 1930, a most unusual visitor paid a visit to Alessandro: Armida Barelli, president of La Gioventù Femminile di Azione Cattolica (Young Women of Catholic Action). The group's membership numbered a million women from every part of Italy. Barelli arrived at the Serenellis' door in the company of Iole Sampaolesi, the regional head of the women's group. Barelli's organization would soon make the official request that Maria Goretti's cause for canonization be opened, and she visited Alessandro with this end in mind. Barelli's meeting with Alessandro became the basis for an article published at the end of that same month in her organization's publication *Squilli di Resurrezione.*

After her meeting with Alessandro, Barelli noted that while he was weary from his years in prison, he also possessed a completely calm mind. He told her that the pain of not being able to keep a job was harsher than any he suffered in prison. Barelli shied away from asking him many questions, thinking it inappropriate. Alessandro told Barelli that he had been blinded by a passion for Maria Goretti. He reminded them that he was a nineteen-year-old at the time he committed his crime. He recalled that Maria had indeed warned him that his soul would be damned, and that even during the physical attack Maria was more concerned with covering her legs than trying to ward off the repeated thrust of the weapon in his hand.

Later, in 1935, as a witness before the church tribunal gathering testimonies related to Maria's life and reputation, Barelli would explain that she visited Alessandro because she wanted to talk with the man who killed the girl the people of Italy revered. She wanted to see him and to hear from him, as he was the only witness to Maria's defense of her virginity. She told the tribunal that this was the only time she talked with Alessandro. She repeated to them Alessandro's own words: "Some crimes are never paid enough."

Satisfied that Alessandro was sincere in his conversion and would not in any way undermine Maria's cause, Barelli published her biography of the saint titled *Maria Goretti*. The book, which was published the same year Barelli met with Alessandro, was a reworking of Father Aurelio's book, intended for her Catholic Action members. Her special edition of Father Aurelio's book omitted details she felt would be too upsetting to the Young Women of Catholic Action, such as the autopsy report. Such details, appropriate to a crime report, were too graphic for hagiography, she felt. Barelli was a good spiritual director, and her purpose was not to frighten virtue into the organization's membership but to reveal its strength.

Meanwhile, trying to find employment certainly tested Alessandro's character. The wife of one landowner worked side by side with him in the fields and tried to tempt him to commit adultery with her. She was heartless enough to remind him that he had once killed a girl who would not allow him what she now offered him. Shocked and disgusted, he rejected her offer. At the end of the day, he handed in his resignation. One bit of good fortune came his way, however. Between 1933 and 1937 he found gainful, if sporadic, employment. Alessandro was hired by a landowner who, knowing him to be an ex-convict, told him he didn't care about the past. He expected only that he work hard and conduct himself properly.

Despite Alessandro's notoriety, Pietro and Maria encouraged him to marry. His brother told him of a woman in the town who was looking for a husband. Pietro was certain that she was not concerned about his past and would surely accept his proposal, should he approach her. Alessandro rejected this idea outright.

The only woman he wanted to see was Assunta Goretti. He wanted to beg her forgiveness.

Assunta Goretti lived just a few miles from Torrette, in Corinaldo, where she worked as the housekeeper for the parish priest. It was this priest, Father Francesco Bernacchio, who arranged a meeting between Alessandro and Assunta.

In 1934, five years after his release, Alessandro accepted the invitation of Father Bernacchio to spend the Christmas holidays with him at his rectory. On Christmas Eve, Alessandro knocked at the rectory door and was greeted by Assunta. Awkwardly, he asked Assunta if she recognized him. With tearful eyes, she assured him she did know him. It had been thirty-two years since he murdered her daughter. Still standing at the threshold, Alessandro asked her if she could forgive him for what he had done — both to Maria and to her. Without hesitation, in words Alessandro would repeat over the years, Assunta said: "God has forgiven you, Maria has forgiven you, and I too forgive you." Both cried and embraced and went to a parlor where they answered each other's questions about the years that had elapsed since they last saw each other. Their last meeting had been thirty-two years earlier, then, in a Roman courtroom — as together they heard the judge pronounce sentence.

On Christmas morning, accompanied by Ersilia, Maria's sister, Assunta and Alessandro attended Mass and knelt beside each other to receive Communion. Sadly, the lasting joy of this special

Christmas with Assunta had to end. Back at his job, Alessandro contracted bronchial pneumonia and was confined to a hospital for forty-five days.

If Alessandro could not find peace among the farmers of the region, he did have the great peace of knowing the Goretti family would not shun him. Rather, they embraced him and were glad of his conversion and his freedom. Still, but for a few short stints, he remained unemployable.

•••

After the 1934 Christmas reunion with the Goretti family, Alessandro would occasionally travel back to Corinaldo, the one place he had found any sense of security or welcome. He visited with Assunta at the home of Maria's sister, Ersilia, and her family. These must have been emotional gatherings.

In 1935, the process of canonization for Maria Goretti opened in the town of Albano. This stage information about the candidate is gathered, often through interviews with those who knew them. Ersilia had little memory of her famous sister, so she would not be slated to testify. Assunta and Alessandro knew they would be called before the tribunal. (Alessandro would testify between 1938 and 1941.) The mother and the murderer knew the difficult memories they would both be called upon to share before the panel of canonical jurists. And, in the case of Alessandro, the advocates would not tread softly.

In 1937, Father Bernacchio realized that he needed, in charity, to intervene in the widespread, unrelenting rejection of Alessandro. Enthusiasm for Maria encouraged many of her devotees to heap disdain on the sinner who killed her. To provide Alessandro some relief and safety, Father Bernacchio asked the Capuchin friars in Amandola if they would allow Alessandro to live among them in exchange for work.

The friars agreed. Alessandro, now fifty-five and still able-bodied, earned his room and board working as porter and gardener at the friary and Marian shrine at Amandola. Even confined within a monastery, however, Alessandro would again be denied peace. In fact, shortly after his arrival, he was jailed again.

An elderly layman worked for the Capuchins in their ancient monastery in its beautiful mountain setting. Like Alessandro, he lived side by side with the friars, occupying the same part of the monastery as Alessandro. This elderly worker felt his job was threatened by Alessandro presence so he schemed to rid the place of his competition. He approached the superior and told him that his hidden savings, amounting to 4,000 lire, had been stolen. He was sure Alessandro was the thief.

The superior, recognizing this to be a criminal offense, sent for the police. The marshal heard each man's account and agreed that Alessandro must surely be the thief. He told Alessandro to walk down the mountainside to the village and turn himself in to the jailer. For fourteen days, Alessandro sat in a cell, knowing all the while that he was innocent.

Eventually, the conscience of the insecure worker moved him to confess. Alessandro was released and returned to the friary, only to be met with the unimaginable: The superior, uncomfortable with the situation, informed Alessandro that he could no longer allow him to stay at Amandola. Dejected, Alessandro returned to Corinaldo.

In 1938, Father Bernacchio again helped Alessandro find a haven. He arranged that another Capuchin friary, this time in nearby Ascoli Piceno, house him in exchange for work in their gardens. It would be from Ascoli Piceno that Alessandro would be called to give testimony and publicly recount his offense as part of the canonization process.

Chapter Five

The Making of a Saint

Even before Alessandro Serenelli was called as a witness, the postulator for Maria Goretti's cause sent out a reconnaissance team. While Armida Barelli's organization petitioned to open the cause, Barelli (whose own cause is now under way) could not serve as postulator. At the time, that position had to be filled by a priest in Rome. So the job of postulator was given to Father Mauro Liberati.

Father Liberati had a personal devotion to Maria Goretti. He had previously served as vice-postulator to his predecessor, the Venerable Father Germanus Ruoppolo. Under Father Ruoppolo's tutorship, Father Liberati assisted with two successful causes: those of Gemma Galgani, a laywoman and stigmatic, and Francis Possenti, a Passionist seminarian known as Gabriel of the Sorrowful Virgin.

Father Liberati wanted to ensure that Alessandro was truly repentant so he sent Father Verticchio and Barelli to conduct unannounced visits to Alessandro before he was summoned as a witness during the canonical trial. Father Verticchio was a Passionist and Maria's official biographer.

In the first week of November 1935, while sowing a winter crop at Osimo, Alessandro was summoned from the field by the landowner for whom he worked at the time. There were three priests who wanted to speak with him. Alessandro recognized one of the priests as the pastor of the parish in Osimo. The second he learned was a chaplain from Corinaldo. The third priest he recognized only by his attire: He wore the habit of the Passionists, the order in charge of the churches in Paliano (where Alessandro had moved to assist his father years ago) and Le Ferriere, where they had lived with the Gorettis. The Passionist, who had a book tucked under his arm, was Father Verticchio. The book was his biography of Maria Goretti.

When a cause is initiated, those proposing the candidate for sainthood must gather biographical information to serve as evidence of their life of virtue and faith. Since the Passionists were supporting the cause (though they did not initiate it), it was logical that a member of their order would gather and write the official biography. The task fell to Father Verticchio. He testified during the ordinary process — the first stage in the lengthy process of canonization — that he had conducted extensive interviews in the locales associated with the Goretti family. He had also consulted the penal records associated with Alessandro's trial and conviction. His finding needed to be objective, free of any prejudice. While the material was collected primarily to assist the postulator charged with advancing or shelving Maria Goretti's cause, it was also intended for publication with the purpose of making Maria more widely known.

The title of Father Verticchio's book, *La S. Agnese del secolo XX — Maria Goretti martire della purità* (*The Saint Agnes of the Twentieth Century — Maria Goretti — Martyr of Purity*), made his view of Maria quite clear. He saw her as a virgin-martyr in the mold of Agnes, Agatha, and Lucy, saints in the early Church who had opted for death rather than renouncing their Christianity or relinquishing their virginity. While Father Verticchio believed Maria was not just murdered but was martyred would have to be established. His biography, published to coincide with the exhumation of Maria's remains in 1929, was a bestseller, going through many printings and a number of translations.

On that November day in 1935, the priests asked the landowner for a place where they could talk privately with Alessandro. At first the unannounced visitors told Alessandro they had just happened by, not planning to meet with him. But they soon realized how foolish this fabricated statement sounded and admitted they were there on serious business. They had come to talk about Maria's cause for sainthood, which had officially opened at the end of May that year. They also wanted to talk about him. They knew Alessandro's conversion story and his good reputation since that experience. Clearly, they wanted to verify for themselves that Alessandro was a good Christian, that he lived in harmony with the Church, and, for their purposes, that he would be a credible witness should he be called to testify before the canonical tribunal at Albano.

Alessandro understood their motive. He and Assunta had discussed the probability of his being called to recount the murder of Maria. A month after the three priests met with Alessandro, he was notified that he would indeed be called as a witness to his victim's death and heroic virtue.

When the tribunal assembled at Albano in 1935 to open the canonical process for Maria's cause, Alessandro was not the first called to make a statement. In fact, he was the twelfth. Obviously, he was the central witness to the events surrounding Maria's death, but the chief proponent of her cause, its postulator, chose to have others speak first. If Maria's cause was to advance, the postulator needed to have everything in order. Thus, Alessandro's testimony would come soon after that of Maria's mother.

At that time there was debate as to the merits of Maria's cause.

As popular as devotion was among the faithful, the Church needed to be thorough. After all, many innocent victims of sexual assault had been tragically killed in similar circumstances, and the tragedy on its own did not make them saints. The Church needed to be certain, first of all, that Maria had resisted her assailant without any hesitation, even momentarily. So at the beginning, Maria herself was on trial. Alessandro's testimony would make or break the case for her innocence.

This cause was truly unique, and the Church, always cautious is such matters, was rigorous in proceeding. One of the names rarely mentioned regarding Maria's cause is Cardinal William Theodore Heard. A Scotsman and a convert to Catholicism, Cardinal Heard lived in Rome at the Venerable English College on the Via di Monserrato. Before he was elevated to the rank of cardinal, one of Heard's duties was to audit and confer on the merits of cases under consideration by the Sacred Congregation of Rites (today called the Sacred Congregation for the Causes of Saints). One of his students at the *Venerabile*, Antony Kenny, provides a brief look at the conversations in which Cardinal Heard took part concerning Maria's case. In his autobiography, *A Path from Rome*, Kenny writes:

> I was impressed by the trouble [Heard] and
> his colleagues took over canonizations. Once,
> while helping to clear his rooms, I found seven

volumes of argument devoted to two words of Maria Goretti, who was eventually canonized as a martyr of chastity. Her last words were *"Si, si."* Were these reinforcing her previous words to her would-be-seducer, namely, *"Dio non vuole"*? Or were they a last-minute surrender to his proposition, too late to ward off the knife? Postulator and *promotor fidei* had argued the case before Heard and his colleagues for many hours.

In 1984, Giordano Bruno Guerri unnerved many of the faithful when he revisited Alessandro's testimony regarding these last words of Maria in his book, *Povera Santa, Povero Assassino: La vera storia di Maria Goretti* (*Poor Saint, Poor Murderer: The True Story of Maria Goretti*). Guerri had no idea that these seven notebooks of Cardinal Heard even existed. These notebooks witnessed to the Church's honesty in deliberating over Maria's cause, including her words spoken to Alessandro while she was under attack. Guerri questioned the integrity of the canonical process that labored over Maria's words. His book attempts to exonerate the murderer of responsibility for his actions due to extreme poverty. Yet *povero* Alessandro testified on Maria's behalf; he told the truth without coercion. It was never a matter of conspiracy. Father Liberati (the postulator) and Cardinal Carlo

Salotti (the *promotor fidei*, commonly called the "devil's advocate," who is charged with defeating the cause) did not collabo-
rate to make Maria's words fit a predetermined popular verdict.
Guerri doesn't accept that both sides sought an objective truth.
Yet both postulator and devil's advocate alike wanted to know
not only what Maria said but, perhaps more importantly, what
Alessandro had understood her words to mean when he heard
them. Alessandro testified that he understood Maria's "No" to
mean "No."

Alessandro was called before the tribunal at Albano between
1938 and 1941. During this period, when needed in Albano, he
would commute to Rome where he stayed with the Passionists
at La Scala Santa in Rome. This church, directly across a piazza
from the Basilica of St. John Lateran, houses the stairs that tradition says Jesus climbed when he was brought before Pontius
Pilate. One of the principal pilgrimage sites in Rome, this church
is the Roman provincial headquarters of the Passionists, and it
was the residence of Father Liberati.

The *positio* records Alessandro's memory of his years of living with his father alongside the Goretti family. He recounted
in detail his harassment of Maria and his murderous actions.
Appended to his testimony were the crude statements he made
to the local police almost forty years earlier, at the time of the
crime, and the findings of the court that determined his sanity
and convicted him. He was thorough and transparent.

Father Liberati realized from the outset that the faithful believed Maria was a martyr. Yet he knew that Maria's murder did not conform to the standard measures of martyrdom. Still, he considered her to be truly a martyr, someone who witnessed to the Faith by her blood. And he knew that, as far back as 1910, Pope Saint Pius X alluded to Maria as a new Saint Agnes. Agnes too was a young girl, and she too had refused to relinquish her virginity for the sake of saving her life. There was an important difference, however: A martyr is one who dies rather than renounce the Faith, or who is killed out of hatred for the Faith, as Agnes ultimately was. Alessandro had not demanded that Maria renounce her faith. He himself was a Catholic, and even as a young man he often attended Sunday Mass and frequently joined in praying the evening Rosary with Assunta and her children after a day's work. Alessandro was not a powerful pagan official, he was a sharecropper just like his victim. His demands had been solely carnal. Yet Maria had preserved her virginal integrity. On July 6, 1902, Francesco Bartoli, the surgeon who headed the team of three that sought to save Maria's life, assured the child's mother that her daughter remained a virgin. Mrs. Goretti would repeat the doctor's assurance that this was so in her testimony at Albano.

While Maria was certainly a virgin, did she really qualify as a martyr? Father Liberati believed she did. Maria had died courageously resisting the violation of her body, which she knew to be a temple of the Holy Spirit. What is more, she was killed while trying to convince her attacker that his sin would have eternal consequences for his own soul. To prove his case, Father Liberati would have to effect a history-making paradigm shift regarding the definition of martyrdom. The *positio* reviews this issue at length, taking into consideration the long-standing opinions of theologians on the matter of martyrdom. The authority cited most in the documents is Saint Thomas Aquinas. Aquinas believed that one could be a martyr by dying for a single Christian virtue. But surprisingly, Father Liberati did not use what might be a more cogent statement supporting his argument. Saint Augustine, writing to a fellow bishop on the subject of chastity challenged by violence, concluded: "Violence cannot violate chastity if the mind preserves it. Even the chastity of the body is not violated when she who suffers is not voluntarily abusing her body but is enduring without consenting to what another is perpetrating." This would have been a strong argument to help prove that Maria, who died while her chastity was violently challenged, was truly a martyr.

On March 25, 1945, Pope Pius XII declared the death of Maria Goretti to be martyrdom. Thus the requirement that two miracles be attributed to her intercession was waived. (At that time, to be beatified two miracles had to be attributed to a candidate's intercession, unless they died as martyrs.) The beatification could be scheduled, and Maria would be officially listed as a virgin-martyr. Unfortunately, the ceremony had to be put off for a time. World War II had wreaked havoc in Italy and in Rome itself, and order needed to be restored before it would be appropriate to proceed. Finally, on April 27, 1947, Maria Goretti was beatified.

The press reported that Alessandro attended the beatification of his victim. This is not the case. He did not attend the beatification, and he would not attend the canonization, either. He explained the reason for his absence from the beatification in interviews he granted sometime after the fact.

The Capuchin Guardian, the head of the friary at Ascoli Piceno where Alessandro lived, wanted Alessandro to attend the beatification. At first, Alessandro thought it best to stay away, and some of the friars concurred. They worried that his presence at the celebration might distract, even detract, from the ceremony. But Alessandro vacillated, and in the end, he decided he would go, but in disguise (he proposed wearing a religious habit and going by an alias). If he were recognized, he feared he would be pointed out as Maria's murderer. In the end, Alessandro was spared the awkwardness of both the disguise hoax and the possibility of being recognized. A couple of days before Alessandro was to journey to Rome, the friar who was to accompany him died. In one interview, Alessandro said the friar died as the result of being accidentally shot. In another, he said simply that the friar had died suddenly. Either way, Alessandro and the friars agreed that this unexpected death should be accepted as a providential sign and that Alessandro should stay home.

In 1950, Maria was canonized in unprecedented fashion. It was a holy year, and large numbers of pilgrims were visiting Rome. The Roman heat was intense, and Pius XII's doctors insisted that he cancel all audiences for days leading up to the canonization. The ceremony spanned two days, and for the first time in history, a canonization would be held in St. Peter's Square. Requests for tickets had come in from all over the world, so the decision had been made to move the ceremony outdoors where an estimated 500,000 people packed the square and the nearby streets to participate. For the first time, too, the mother of the newly canonized would be present.

Alessandro, then sixty-eight, was not there. Instead, he chose to join the friars in listening to the ceremony on the radio at Ascoli Piceno.

Alessandro Serenelli later in life. Copyright Fr. Carlos Martins.

Chapter Six

Life after Albano: Prayer, Penance, and Waiting

After Alessandro gave his testimony on behalf of Maria's cause, he returned to Ascoli Piceno. There he resumed his duties as gardener and porter. He would spend eighteen years at Ascoli Piceno, occasionally leaving when called on to present himself before the tribunal. For the most part, these eighteen years were a time of long-awaited peace.

When he first came to live at Ascoli Piceno, the curious came to see if they could glimpse this infamous man. As porter, for years he opened the door at which they knocked. Frequently, bold visitors would ask him if it was true that the murderer of Maria Goretti lived in the friary. He would answer that it was indeed true. When asked what he was like and what he did there, Alessandro would respond that he was just like himself and did exactly the same work as he. Eventually, these unwanted intrusions into his daily life became rare. Later, people sought him out through letters (but as we shall see, these would be very different in their aim).

Remember that Alessandro had spent twenty-seven years in prison. When at last he was set free, he lived as a vagabond, unable to find lasting work or peace. For this reason, the friary was more than just shelter to Alessandro; it provided him with a sense of stability and rest. It suited him. While a prison and a friary are radically different, they have some aspects in common. Both are home to a single-sex population, and both depend on a fixed schedule, allowing the occupants to move through the day in order and peace.

Though Alessandro never became a Capuchin friar, and there doesn't seem to be any hint that he ever felt inclined to do so, he did participate fully in the daily routine of the friary. He followed both the work regimen and the *horarium*, the prayer schedule of the community. In his free time, he pursued his love for reading and availed himself of the community's library of both spiritual and secular books. In time, Alessandro joined the secular Capuchin Third Order, but he always remained a layman.

Over the years of his stay at Ascoli Piceno, the public's attitude toward Alessandro came to change. The friars, who shared their lives with him in their community, also shared their lives with those outside the friary walls. Unlike enclosed or cloistered monks, Capuchins minister in society. At Ascoli Piceno, the friars staff a church, which then and now serves much like a parish church, where they celebrated Mass, heard confessions, preached, and provided spiritual direction. In turn, and in keeping with the tradition of their order, they depended on the generosity of their neighbors for their material support.

Because of the friars' relationships with the local community, over time word spread of Alessandro's life of prayer and repentance. It is likely that the friars answered questions about Alessandro when asked by those with whom they came into daily contact. Gradually, people came to view Alessandro with less and less suspicion. As he was gradually entrusted with chores outside the friary walls, the local population came to know firsthand that the "monster," by God's grace, had become a trustworthy man of character. They knew of his great devotion to Maria. They knew he believed that she, having forgiven him before her own life ended, now accompanied him on his own journey toward death.

Over time, Alessandro also began to receive prayer requests

from near and far. He was a man of prayer and repentance, and it became part of his vocation to pray on behalf of others, particularly to Maria, his own intercessor.

He made very few excursions away from Ascoli Piceno. In 1950, shortly after Maria's canonization, Alessandro visited the house at Le Ferriere di Conca where he and his father had lived alongside the Goretti family. To enter the house, one climbs a long outside brick stairway and walks directly into the kitchen. This was a common kitchen, shared by both families. It was in fact the only part of the house not given over to bedrooms, and perhaps is best described as a family room. In this room, right at the door, Alessandro had plunged the sharpened awl into his victim for a second round of stabbings. Here Maria had warned him of the gravity of the sin he proposed, less concerned for her own life than for the salvation of his soul. Surely this visit, forty-eight years after the murder, stirred great emotion in him. Pointing to the spot where Maria collapsed, he said simply to the Passionist priest who accompanied him, "I murdered her here." He sobbed and wept.

In June 1954, Alessandro, now seventy-two years old, again ventured out of Ascoli Piceno. This time he traveled to Corinaldo to visit Assunta Goretti, who was failing. They sat, she now in a wheelchair, and spoke at length. At their parting, they embraced as always. This was to be the last time they would meet.

Maria's sister, Ersilia, had always welcomed Alessandro into her home, where her mother lived along with her own family. Since the Christmas reunion of 1934, the home was always open to him. In early October 1954, Ersilia sent a telegram to the friary alerting Alessandro that her mother's death was imminent. He set out for Corinaldo at once. He intended to be with Assunta and her family at the end. On his arrival, however, he found that she had already died.

Alessandro was now showing signs of age. Assessing his condition, the Passionist's Guardian decided to transfer him from Ascoli Piceno to the friary at Macerata, home to elderly and sick friars. Alessandro arrived at Macerata on November 17, 1956.

Until just months before his death, Alessandro remained an active member of his new community. The daily routine, particularly his workload, was less difficult. The community followed a similar prayer rhythm to that of Ascoli Piceno, and he participated fully in daily Mass and the various offices chanted several times each day. Like aging religious everywhere, the work assigned to the aged friars is spiritual: to pray for the Church, and particularly for those friars still active in the order's apostolates. Alessandro did as the friars did, adding special devotional prayers to Maria for himself and for those who requested his prayers.

Age was clearly overtaking Alessandro. At Macerata a young friar, Brother Mario Pacchiarini, was assigned as his caregiver and remained so until the end. At this point, Alessandro had been using a cane for some years and was becoming less and less steady on his feet. On his way to the chapel for one of the offices in February 1970, he fell and broke his right femur. He was taken to the hospital, where the injury was found to be inoperable because of his advanced age. This was the advent of Alessandro's decline.

Chapter Seven

Requiescat in Pace (1970)

The death of Alessandro Serenelli did not escape the press. He died peacefully on May 6, 1970, in a sparsely furnished cell in the friary's infirmary. When word of "the monster's" imminent death reached the public, the media leapt to cover it. Father Urbano, the guardian of the friary at Macerata, let a number of journalists visit the dying Alessandro. Among them was Dino Satriano, a reporter for *Gente*, a popular "Weekly of Politics, News and Culture." He detailed his visit in a two-page spread complete with a photo of the dying man. The article appeared just sixteen days before Alessandro's death.

Satriano headlined his story, "The Killer of Maria Goretti is Dying like a Saint." His sub-headline was a quote from Alessandro: "I am leaving quietly if everyone has forgiven me." The journalist described the state of Alessandro's health, and the gentle care with which the friars attended him. The friars confided that they found it hard to accept that Alessandro was truly at death's door. But Alessandro himself said he was ready to die, "to finally reach my Marietta, waiting for me in paradise." Satriano described the scene: "And his eyes turn to the table on which there are two images of Maria Goretti and a stack of holy cards that he has signed with his own neat handwriting, to send to people from all over the world who have written."

The friars showed the journalist a parcel of letters and postcards with messages like: "Alessandro, pray to Saint Maria Goretti for me." "Intercede with your Marietta to save my dying child." "Only you can ask the little martyr for this grace." "As you have a loved one close to God, pray for the healing of my mother." The friars explained that these messages of pain and hope, more than anything else, had helped Alessandro to believe in his own redemption, and to forget the time when he was, for all, nothing but a "monster."

Satriano reported that when Alessandro's pain intensified, and a complaint escaped him, he would immediately repeat, "Patience, patience" and, "We thank God." Brother Gilberto assured the journalist regarding his confrere's ongoing pain: "It is atrocious suffering. It is real martyrdom, yet he is the one who gives courage to us. He has the strength and resignation of a saint. For ourselves he is an example of faith, of complete trust in the work of the Lord." The interview was interrupted by the arrival of a telegram addressed to Alessandro, which was read aloud to him: "I ask your blessing and your prayers to save my family from a desperate situation."

Father Urbano concluded the *Gente* interview, by telling the reporter: "How many times over all these years people came to him saying, 'Blessed are you who will go to heaven because Maria Goretti has promised it to you.' And he would always reply, 'It is not true, it is not true, because one has to deserve paradise.'"

"I believe, however," Father Urbano said, speaking for himself, "that he truly deserves paradise."

Alessandro Serenelli, the criminal, served a prison sentence. After his conversion, recognizing that he had sinned gravely, he consigned himself to a life of prayer and penance. Yet he never believed he was on his own. He was confident that, by the grace of God, Maria accompanied him throughout his life.

Just two weeks after Alessandro's death, the Italian weekly *Alba* printed an article announcing, "The Murderer of Maria Goretti died in Peace." The writer, Dino Antonini, related that Alessandro's last words were that he was looking forward to seeing "Marietta" again. Antonini wrote that if Maria Goretti is a symbol of innocence, Alessandro should be considered a symbol of the truly repented. He shunned the spotlight: "He was never happy to grant interviews, never sought publicity, not even to let people know he was sorry." Maria's example is a powerful part of *their* story, but so too is Alessandro's witness: "It is also the example of the murderer who has expiated, suffered, and rejected publicity. A brute who has redeemed himself."

In the United States, a lengthy obituary appeared in the tabloid *National Enquirer*. Since 1926, the tabloid has catered to Americans' appetite for gossip. Shortly after Alessandro's death, it printed a surprisingly un-torrid account of his life. The article, headlined "Murderer Whose Victim Became a Saint Dies After 68 Years of Penance," emphasized Alessandro's repentance (though it did not include any reference to the dream that occasioned his conversion). The article underscored the sad reality that, once released from prison, Alessandro was "taunted and reviled" wherever he tried to settle. The report did contain some minor factual errors. For example, even though by 1970 it was well established that Alessandro had not attended Maria's canonization, *National Enquirer* reported, "In the crowd when the pope proclaimed Maria a saint was Alessandro, who had come to be known by the Italians as 'the monster.'"

Following his death, Alessandro was coming to be appreciated as a genuinely holy man. In America, the *National Enquirer* took note of this. Its reporter wrote: "As the years passed, Alessandro became deaf, almost blind and was stricken with arthritis and rheumatism. Word of his devotion to the little saint spread and people from all over the world began asking the old man to include them in his prayers."

Maria was held in the highest esteem from the moment of her death. Her cult was spontaneous. Ordinary people, from far beyond the marshes where she lived and died, were quick to appreciate that her resistance to rape was courageous. Courage, like chastity, is a virtue, and it is numbered among the gifts of the Holy Spirit. Maria's refusal to cooperate with her attacker was based, according to her own words, on her choice not to cooperate with a sinner, but to stand up to her assailant. In her attempt to change Alessandro's mind, she didn't say, "No, no, no! It is a sin, *we* will go to hell." She warned him, "You will go to hell." She remained chaste to the end, yes, but she knew that no matter what might transpire in the kitchen that Saturday afternoon, she would not be in danger of damnation. One gets the impression that Maria was steeled against sin of any kind and would have refused to cooperate with Alessandro had he merely suggested they steal a neighbor's chicken to alleviate their household's hunger.

In 2010, the bishop of Macerata (where Alessandro was buried alongside Capuchin friars in their crypt) and the bishop of Senigallia decided to relocate Alessandro's remains. Today, they rest in the wall of the church dedicated to Maria in Corinaldo. He is buried just to the right of the entrance to the church, directly across from the tomb of Assunta Goretti.

After Alessandro's death, a letter he had written dated May 5, 1961, was discovered among his belongings. It reads as follows:

> I am nearly 80 years old. I am about to depart.
>
> Looking back at my past, I can see that in my early youth, I chose a bad path which led me to ruin myself.
>
> My behavior was influenced by print, mass-media, and bad examples which are followed by the majority of young people without ever thinking. And I did the same. I was not worried.
>
> There were a lot of generous and devoted people who surrounded me, but I paid no attention to them because a violent force blinded me and pushed me toward a wrong way of life.
>
> When I was 20 years old, I committed a crime of passion. Now, that memory represents something horrible for me. Maria Goretti, now a Saint, was my good angel, sent to me through Providence to guide and save me. I still have impressed upon my heart her words of rebuke and pardon. She prayed for me, she interceded for her murderer. Thirty years of prison followed.

If I had been of age, I would have spent all my life in prison. I accepted to be condemned because it was my own fault.

Marietta was really my light, my protectress; with her help, I behaved well during the 27 years of prison and tried to live honestly when I was again accepted among members of society. Franciscan friars, Capuchins from the Marche, welcomed me with angelic charity into their monastery as a brother, not as a servant. I have been living with their community for 24 years and now I am serenely waiting to witness the vision of God, to hug my loved ones again, and to be next to my Guardian Angel and her dear mother, Assunta.

I hope this letter that I wrote can teach others the happy lesson of avoiding evil and of always following the right path, like little children. I feel that religion with its precepts is not something we can live without, but rather it is the real comfort, the real strength in life and the only safe way in every circumstance, even the most painful ones of life.

Relief of Maria Goretti and Alessandro Serenelli, Basilica of the National Shrine of the Immaculate Conception. Saint Maria Goretti (1976), Theodore C. Barbarossa. © Basilica of the National Shrine of the Immaculate Conception, Washington, D.C.

Epilogue

A Cult of One's Own

Today, "the monster's" cult is growing. It will grow slowly, and it will meet with opposition.

In a small Catholic Truth Society booklet titled *The Canonization of Saints*, Monsignor P. E. Hallett points out that "whilst we are at liberty privately to venerate and invoke the intercession of any one whom we may think to be in heaven, the Church will not allow any act that betokens religious honor or *cultus* to be paid publicly to anyone whom she has not declared 'blessed.'" The Church reserves to herself the prerogative of canonization, or the listing of the names of the saints. She also — and with good reason — limits how the non-canonized faithful departed may be memorialized. Saints are canonized usually after a long process, during which every aspect of their thoughts, words, deeds, and reputation are thoroughly scrutinized. Then and only then is a public *cultus* approved.

Those conducting the investigation leading up to canonization must take their time. They must listen to both sides, those promoting the candidate for sainthood and those opposed. When all is said and done, those promoting the saint-to-be must demonstrate that he or she witnessed heroic virtue during life. Heroic virtue, at heart, means that a particular Gospel value motivated the saint, and was visibly lived out in his or her life. It is the spark of a saint's *cultus*.

Over the years since her death, Maria Goretti has won the affection and devotion of many. Much has been written about her, detailing her tragic story. But there is more to say, because Maria's story is also Alessandro's story. Because this is so, Maria is a saint for adults, much more than she is a saint for children, the audience to whom she was very often presented. I believe, in fact, she can only be fully appreciated by those who have moved beyond childhood. Over the years, those who have told her story have been appropriately uncomfortable detailing it for young readers, their target audience in most cases. The young do not yet have the life experience or critical skills needed to grasp such details.

In fact, Saint Maria Goretti is one of the most controversial saints, because in telling her story some have arguably made her one dimensional. She is presented as having only one case to make: the unpopular case for untainted chastity, so readily ridiculed in today's popular culture. Maria was unquestionably chaste, and this was identified as her heroic virtue by those who canonized her. Yet in focusing on this virtue, Maria's biographies portray her more as a stop sign for young people, rather than a sure way to follow. How are we meant to imitate Maria's example of holiness? In order to answer this question, we must discover a Maria Goretti of even greater value and wider appeal.

To speak of Maria Goretti is also to speak of Alessandro Serenelli, and this requires a more frank and less reserved narrative. Maria is indeed pure. The young Alessandro clearly was not — he stands as her stark antithesis. Clearly, she was motivated by grace; he rejected that gift. In order to present both stories well, we need to be less puritanical in telling *their* story, which requires mature and transparent language, not the guarded vocabulary used in earlier tellings. A freer use of the primary sources allows for this, and in the course of examining these sources, we find Maria as much a saint of mercy and forgiveness as she is a saint of purity. With this less censored look, we might also see Maria as an extraordinary model of accompaniment. Alessandro was convinced, from the day he awoke after the dream in which he came to his senses, that she was and would remain his greatest advocate. She proved this not just during his attack on her purity, but throughout the rest of his life until his own peaceful death. This story is not just hers or his: It is *their* story.

Though devotion to Alessandro is nascent, there are already a number of expressions of it, even in America. Why? Alessandro is, after all, the villain of the story. Yet as early as the beatification of Maria Goretti, it was clear that her admittance to the catalog of saints was to a degree made possible by her murderer's repentance. Alessandro's conversion awed many. More awe-inspiring, if such things can be quantified, was Maria's desire that he be with her one day in heaven. Had Alessandro never converted, Maria's words of pardon would still have provoked our admiration. But when it comes to canonizing saints, the Church also wants miracles, as these are demonstrations from God that it is his will that we should add a name to the canon of saints.

Pietro Di Donato wrote a book on Alessandro, *The Penitent*, in 1962. Sometimes referred to as a novel because of the author's free use of dialogue, it is the only full-length account of Alessandro's life in English. Published eight years before its subject's death, it remains an unfinished telling of his life. Missing are the details of Alessandro's last years. Missing too are the details of a growing appreciation for the full effect of his conversion, especially among those who encountered him. Di Donato's book did provide a picture of a truly remorseful man, one confident of his own salvation. Alessandro had killed a saint. He concluded his meeting with the author saying: "Each night in this tiny room, I put out the light, and pray to my saint, my Marietta. I pray, waiting, that the promise the little girl made on her deathbed, to receive me in paradise, will be accomplished." The book is cultic in that it did give its readers some evidence of the effect of grace on its subject. However, this book did not introduce Alessandro to the reading public; instead, the many books about Maria Goretti did. Unlike those books, Di Dinato's book invited readers to see Alessandro in a more sympathetic light.

In the autumn of 1979, New York-based journalist Ann Plogsterth, writing for the *National Catholic Reporter*, penned a column headlined "Goretti's attacker: A Saint?" Writing from a Catholic and feminist point of view, it was her own experience of being a woman tourist in Italy that occasioned the reflection. Plogsterth observes, "The fate of her attacker is also instructive." She concludes her article saying: "He died in 1970, an example that true conversion of life is never impossible. To me he seems as suitable a candidate for canonization as was his little victim."

For many years, Maryknoll Brother Goretti Zilli has been associated with promoting his namesake. Zilli was born in the Bronx, New York, in 1934. From 1954 to 1957 he served in the United States Army, chiefly as a cook. In 1957 he entered Maryknoll, a mission society whose founders were imprisoned by the communists for their efforts to reinvigorate the Gospel to China.

Brother Goretti Zilli honors his namesake with fervor. He

established the Maria Goretti Center at Ossining, New York, the Maryknoll headquarters, and he was the moving force behind the film *Love's Bravest Choice,* produced in 2000. The film is described as the "Story of the Young and Courageous Saint Maria Goretti. A docudrama of St. Maria Goretti's life — Role model for teenagers. An inspiration for people everywhere." Brother Zilli also had holy cards printed using different images of Maria and has disseminated them widely.

He also recognizes the worthiness of Alessandro Serenelli. As of the writing of this book, he has begun looking into the feasibility of producing a film on Alessandro. He promotes Alessandro as an example of the power of forgiveness accepted. It was knowledge of Maria's having forgiven him that brought about Alessandro's transformation. Later, the forgiveness extended by Assunta Goretti and Maria's brothers and sisters determined his resolve to spend his remaining years in prayer and repentance, and in promoting devotion to Maria.

Perhaps the most prominent proponent of the cult of Alessandro in America, however, is Father Carlos Martins, a Canadian and member of the Companions of the Cross. Father Martins identifies himself as a convert from atheism. He works with university students and serves as the postulator for the cause of the founders of the Companions of the Cross. He also devotes his energies to a ministry centered on relics, called Treasures of the Church. Through talks and expositions, Martins' ministry helps people understand and appreciate the role of relics in the Church's life. Traveling with dozens of relics to parishes throughout the United States, Father Martins provides the opportunity for people to venerate the sacred remains of saints, some ancient, some more recently canonized. At the conclusion of his presentation, Father Martins focuses in depth on the life and miracles of one saint in particular: Maria Goretti. He tells her story, explaining the circumstances leading up to her murder. Unlike most of the written accounts of Maria Goretti and Alessandro, Martins' presentation provides details of the violence and its aftermath.

While describing the murder, Father Martins holds a facsimile of the murder weapon, displaying it as he describes the horror Maria must have known on realizing that any possibility of an escape was gone. That Maria received fourteen wounds is well-known. Father Martins tells us more. The weapon used, not a knife but a six-inch awl, punctured rather than tore. Had it been a knife, Maria may not have lived beyond the attack. We hear which parts of the child's body were wounded and, in some cases, the depth of the awl's penetration.

During her last hours in the hospital, the probing of these wounds and sutures used to close them added to the child's agony. The doctors used no anesthesia, fearing it would worsen her condition. These graphic details portray the sheer brutality of "the monster," making Maria's ready forgiveness all the more inexplicable.

Father Martins, whose devotion to Maria is palpable, is also a devotee of Alessandro. He displays unabashed respect for the spiritual healing that transformed a hardened murderer, especially for the grace accepted by a man who seemed irredeemable. There are, however, two aspects of Martins' presentation which seem more speculative than factual. First, he says of Alessandro's attempt to rape Maria that "the more it frightened her, the more he liked it." Maybe, but this cannot be historically verified. Second, while we know Maria was heard to pray while enduring pain on the operating table, Father Martins says she offered it for the salvation of sinners. Again, while this is very possible, the evidence remains unsubstantiated.

In 2015, Pope Francis declared a jubilee year, to be centered on God's mercy. During this holy year, Catholics were invited to avail themselves of extraordinary graces and indulgences. During this year, Father Carlos Martins undertook a herculean task: He arranged to bring the wax effigy concealing the bones of Maria Goretti from its shrine in Nettuno, Italy, to the United States. The story of Maria and Alessandro, a story of mercy and forgiveness, provided a beautiful demonstration of the effects of mercy. The tour of Maria's relics was called "The Pilgrimage of Mercy," and it reversed a long-standing paradigm: Instead of requiring pilgrims to make a journey to the site associated with a sacred event or holy person, this pilgrimage brought the relics to the pilgrims.

On the relic tour website, Father Martins said that the Holy See wanted the "Pilgrimage of Mercy" to serve two purposes: First, it was intended to be a spiritual experience for Americans. Second, the tour was to be an opportunity for Americans to show mercy toward Saint Maria. How? By contributing funds for the restoration of the Passionist shrine-church in Nettuno and the house where Maria and Alessandro lived in Le Ferriere. On the Pilgrimage of Mercy website, Father Martins published the combined cost for restoring both sites: $2,062,000. Of that amount, $20,000 was earmarked to turn Alessandro's bedroom into a shrine. There could be no better demonstration of a nascent cult than the readying of a sacred site for his devotees to visit. As of 2018, however, Alessandro's room was inconspicuously marked "the room of the murderer." Still, Father Martins says of Alessandro: "I believe he too one day will be a canonized saint."

Six months after the Pilgrimage of Mercy ended, an article appeared in *America* magazine, written by Raymond P. Roden, a priest of the Diocese of Brooklyn. The article, "An Astounding Mercy: The conversion of the man who killed St. Maria Goretti," speaks specifically about the role mercy played in the conversion of Alessandro. In it, Father Roden recounts how he first came to know the story of Maria and Alessandro, and how, when growing up, he saw their story as a "pious folk tale." On just two pages, Roden reviews the tragic story, makes a case for the importance of forgiveness in our lives, and adds his voice to the small but growing chorus of Alessandro devotees: "I hope that Alessandro Serenelli will come to be known by more people, particularly those tempted to despair because of whatever failures they might feel engulfed by. … The mystical encounter between Maria Goretti and Alessandro Serenelli following her death suggests the possibility of a post-modern asceticism inviting prayer and meditation. Approaching these two friends of God together can offer hope, healing and peace to those who need them most."

At each stop of the Pilgrimage of Mercy tour, visitors received two holy cards. One was a third-class relic, a holy card of Maria painted in the 1920s. The second was a photograph of Alessandro at prayer in his monastic room before a picture of the girl he murdered. Though it has been touched to a handwritten letter penned by Alessandro, it is not a relic of any class. Printed on its reverse is a prayer, to be prayed in "private" devotion, for the canonization of Alessandro Serenelli.

•••

There are several impressive artistic renderings of *their* story. Some, while created to honor Saint Maria Goretti, also include her murderer. The earliest such image is located in Nettuno. Once housed in the Passionist church there, along with Maria's relics, the image dates from 1904, just two years after Maria's death. This imposing monument was erected long before there was any talk of canonization of the young girl, which was unusual if not unprecedented. The church at Nettuno has been renovated several times, and the monument is now housed in the attached museum. It was the idea of a newspaper editor, Enrico Filiziani.

In 1902, *La Vera Roma* published an appeal for funds to erect a monument to the recently murdered Maria. The monument was originally planned for the municipal cemetery where she was buried in Nettuno. The appeal received an impressive response, with donations from Italians at home, and from the Italian diaspora. Much of the funding came from young sodalists of the *Figlie di Maria* — the Children of Mary. Girls from this sodality at St. Anthony of Padua Parish in Greenwich Village, the heart of New York City's "Little Italy," forwarded their contribution.

The monument, an imposing marble memorial using both high and low relief, created by sculptor Raffaele Zaccagnini, is the first portrait created of Maria. It also includes the first image of Alessandro. The image of the wounded victim in the foreground appears almost three dimensional. Above the wounded figure, Maria is shown again, taken heavenward in a swirl of clouds. In the lower right, we see the figure of Alessandro, his back to us, retreating to his room after the attack.

The Basilica of the National Shrine of the Immaculate Conception in Washington, D.C., contains a mezzo-relievo of Saint Maria Goretti, which also includes Alessandro. The relief was carved by Theodore Barbarossa, a native of Vermont. It depicts Maria wearing a long-sleeved dress with its hem extending just below her knees. In her right arm she holds a bouquet of flowers; in her left hand, she holds a single flower stem. In the lower register of the relief, Alessandro is represented in profile, seen from the waist up. His empty right hand is reaching up toward the flower Maria is offering him. The relief is important in that it captures Alessandro's dream. A third of the marble panel is given over to the figure of the assailant in his moment of conversion. Alessandro holds his forehead with his left hand and, as if in shame, tilts his face downward rather than up at his victim.

The Shrine of Our Lady of Guadalupe in La Crosse, Wisconsin, contains another artistic rendering of Maria and Alessandro. The shrine, dedicated in 2008, contains a side chapel dedicated to Saint Maria Goretti. The chapel houses a large altarpiece, painted in oils on linen by Noah Buchanan. Oblong in shape, it rises eleven feet above the altar table and measures four and a half feet across. The painting is divided into two registers almost equal in size. The upper register shows Our Lady set against a radiant sky. Her right hand is raised in blessing, and she looks straight out at the viewer. Immediately in front of Our Lady stands Maria; her face is turned toward the viewer, but she gazes downward to the figure of Alessandro. He is shown kneeling, shirtless, wearing wrist and ankle manacles linked together by heavy chains. He is in his prison cell at Noto. Somewhat embellished by the inclusion of the Blessed Virgin Mary, Buchanan's painting captures the dream that changed his life. The only natural light in the lower register of the La Crosse altarpiece can be seen through the bars of Alessandro's cell window. The truly illuminating light in the lower register comes from the glow of lilies as they turn to small flames in Alessandro's grasp.

Alessandro's place in the La Crosse altarpiece, like his inclusion in the relief in Washington, signals the conversion of the sinner toward the status of saint. Maria's forgiveness, prayers, and accompaniment were the beginnings of her murderer's own cooperation with grace and provided the faithful a glimpse of the spiritual bond that Maria hoped to forge: "I forgive him and I want him to be with me in heaven."

Yet while it has always been their *story*, it has never been their cult. One day they may be so linked — should Alessandro's popular cult advance to a cause. Expect it. Pray for it, that God may be glorified in his angels and in his saints.

Acknowledgments

No book of this kind, no matter how slender the volume, can go without being fattened-up by the addition of a page or two of thank-yous.

My thanks to Brother Goretti Zilli, MM, for sharing his story with me and for providing me with a photocopy of the *positio*, the primary source for all research into the story of Maria Goretti and Alessandro Serenelli.

To Sister Ancilla Matter, FSGM, of the staff of the Shrine of Our Lady of Guadalupe, La Crosse, Wisconsin, for obtaining permission for me to use the photo of the altarpiece depicting Maria and Alessandro at the shrine.

Special thanks to Father Giovanni Alberti, with whom I

have corresponded over a number of years and who I had the pleasure to meet in 2018 in the museum dedicated to Maria Goretti attached to her shrine in Nettuno.

Thanks to two friends and fellow holy card collectors: to Anthony Lentini for help with a number of translations assuring my better understanding of his native language, and to Tom Gilmartin whose technology skills proved a great help.

To Father Raymond P. Roden for permission to quote from his article "An Astounding Mercy."

An especially warm thank you to Sister Miriam and Sister Francesca, custodians of the House of Pardon in Corinaldo, Italy for the warm welcome they extended my wife and me on our 2018 visit to the tomb of Alessandro, now housed in Corinaldo.

Appreciation and thanks to Gofreddo Samory, resident of Corinaldo for guiding us through the sites associated with the early life of Maria in that beautiful hilltop city. His is a deep appreciation for the converted Alessandro, which is inspiring.

Thanks to Dr. Geraldine M. Rohling, archivist and curator of the Basilica of the National Shrine of the Immaculate Conception, Washington, D.C., for permission to use the image of the relief there depicting both Maria and Alessandro.

And, of course, a thank you to Mary Beth Baker, senior acquisitions editor at Our Sunday Visitor. She saw the possible good that bringing this story forward at this time might have, encouraged me, and then supported my approach to allow both the repugnant and the repentant Alessandro to speak for himself.

Bibliography

Antonini, Dino. "The Murderer of Maria Goretti Died in Peace."
Alba, May 21-24, 1970.

Balducci, G. "Una piccolo eroine." *La Figlia di Maria,* December
1902.

Blaher, O.F.M., Damian Joseph. *The Ordinary Process in Causes
of Beatification and Canonization: A Historical Synopsis and
a Commentary.* Washington, DC: The Catholic University of
America Press, 1949.

Brent, Allen. *The Imperial Cult and the Development of Church*

Order. The Netherlands: Brill, 1999.

Brown, Peter. *The Cult of the Saints: Its Rise and Function in Latin Christianity.* Chicago: University of Chicago Press, 1982.

Ciomei, CP, Fortunato. *Il Pugnale Dei Rimorsi.* Nettuno: Santuario di N. S. Delle Grazie e di S. Maria Goretti, 1988.

DiDonato, Pietro. *The Penitent.* New York: Hawthorne, 1962.

Evans, Hal. "Murderer Whose Victim Became a Saint Dies After 68 Years of Penance." *National Enquirer,* 1970.

Francis, Pope. *Evangelii Gaudium.* Vatican City: Libreria Editrice Vaticana, 2013.

Guerri, Giordano Bruno. *Povera Santa Povera Assassino.* Milan: Mondadori, 1985.

Hallitt, P. E. *Canonization of Saints.* London: Catholic Truth Society, 1952.

Hoare, F. R. *The Western Fathers.* New York: Sheed and Ward, 1954.

John Paul II, Pope. "Letter to the Bishop of Albano on the Centenary of the Death of St. Maria Goretti, July 6, 2002." Vatican City: Libreria Editrice Vaticana, 2002.

Kenny, Antony. *A Path from Rome.* Oxford: Oxford University Press, 1985.

Marini, Carlo. *Cenni Biografici della Dodicene Maria Goretti.* Rome: Vera Roma, 1904.

Martins, CC, Carlos. "Sacred Relics and Saints — Treasures of the Church." *DVD*, 2015.

McGuire, RSCJ, Mother CE. *Saint Maria Goretti — Martyr of Purity.* New York: Catholic Book Publishing Co., 1950

Plogsterth, Ann. "Goretti attacker: A Saint?" *National Catholic Reporter,* Sept. 28, 1979.

Rodman, Raymond P. "An Astounding Mercy." *America,* May 2, 2016.

Sacred Congregation of Rites. *Beatificationis Seu Declarationis Martyrii Servae Dei Mariae Goretti Virginis.* Rome: Guerra and Belli, 1938.

Saint John Chrysostom. *The Cult of the Saints.* Yonkers: St. Vladimir's Seminary Press, 2006.

Salmannsperger, H. "Loves Bravest Choice." *VCR*, 2000.

Satriano, Dino. "The Killer of Maria Goretti is Dying Like a Saint." *Gente,* April 20, 1970.

About the Author

Charles D. Engel spent 25 years in Catholic education in the Archdiocese of New York as both a teacher and principal. He holds a B.A. in philosophy and art history and an M.A. in religious studies. He has a lifelong devotion to Saint Maria Goretti and has collected a great deal of material about her: books and pamphlets, newspaper and magazine articles, sacramentals, videos, and more. He visited a number of European and United States archives to research for the writing of this book. Chuck and his wife, Imelda, make their home in Manhattan.

About the Author

Charles B. ... has spent 25 years in Catholic education in the Archdiocese of New York as both a teacher and principal. He holds a B.A. in philosophy and art history, and an M.A. in religious studies. He has a lifelong devotion to Saint Marie Goretti and has collected a great deal of material about her, books and pamphlets, newspaper and magazine articles, so material, videos, and more. He opened a number of European and United States archives to research for the writing of this book. Charles and his wife, Lorelai, make their home in Manhattan.